THE SUBTLE ART OF NOT GIVING A #@%!
JOURNAL

"The opposite of every other book. Don't try. Give up. Be wrong. Lower your standards. Stop believing in yourself. Follow the pain. Each point is profoundly true, useful, and more powerful than the usual positivity. Succinct but surprisingly deep, I read it in one night."

—Derek Sivers, founder of CD Baby and author of *Anything You Want: 40 Lessons for a New Kind of Entrepreneur*

"Resilience, happiness, and freedom come from knowing what to care about and—most important—what not to care about. This is a masterful, philosophical, and practical book that will give readers the wisdom to be able to do just that."

—Ryan Holiday, *New York Times* bestselling author of *The Obstacle Is the Way* and *Ego Is the Enemy*

"Mark Manson is a master of thought-provoking and counterintuitive insights. His easy-to-read style will have you turning pages for hours."

—James Clear, *New York Times* bestselling author of *Atomic Habits*

"An in-your-face guide to living with integrity and finding happiness in sometimes-painful places. . . . This book, full of counterintuitive suggestions that often make great sense, is a pleasure to read and worthy of rereading. A good yardstick by which self-improvement books should be measured."

—*Kirkus Reviews*

THE SUBTLE ART OF NOT GIVING A #@%! JOURNAL

MARK MANSON

HARPER DESIGN
An Imprint of HarperCollins Publishers

Also by Mark Manson

The Subtle Art of Not Giving a Fuck

Everything Is Fucked

Models: Attract Women Through Honesty

THROUGHOUT MY LIFE, I HAVE GIVEN A FUCK ABOUT MANY THINGS, AND I HAVE NOT GIVEN A FUCK ABOUT MANY THINGS . . .

. . . AND IT IS THE *FUCKS NOT GIVEN* THAT HAVE MADE ALL THE DIFFERENCE.

THE SUBTLE ART OF NOT GIVING A F*CK JOURNAL.

Copyright © 2022 by Mark Manson.

All rights reserved. No part of this book may be used or reproduced in any manner whatsoever without written permission except in the case of brief quotations embodied in critical articles and reviews. For information, address HarperCollins Publishers, 195 Broadway, New York, NY 10007.

HarperCollins books may be purchased for educational, business, or sales promotional use. For information, please email the Special Markets Department at SPsales@harpercollins.com.

First published in 2022 by
Harper Design
An Imprint of HarperCollins *Publishers*
195 Broadway
New York, NY 10007
Tel: (212) 207-7000
Fax: (855) 746-3023
harperdesign@harpercollins.com
www.hc.com

Distributed throughout the world by
HarperCollins *Publishers*
195 Broadway
New York, NY 10007

ISBN 978-0-06-322825-2

ISBN 978-0-06-324396-5 (merch edition)

Design by Paul Kepple and Alex Bruce at Headcase Design based on the original by M-80 Design.

Printed in the United States of America

24 25 26 27 28 LBC 8 7 6 5 4

THIS JOURNAL IS THE PROPERTY OF

Courtney hoff

CONTACT

♡ yo mama house ☺ ♡

(If found, please give a fuck and do the right thing!)

Duhhh....

CONTENTS

Introduction 10

Part I: The Warm-Up 15

Part II: Managing Negative Emotions 33

Part III: Better Problems 63

Part IV: Giving Fewer Fucks 85

Part V: Find Greater Purpose 115

A Few Pages of Space to Write Down
Various Personal Realizations 176

Acknowledgments 190

INTRODUCTION

I wrote The Subtle Art of Not Giving a F*ck to be a different kind of self-help book. I didn't want to talk about positivity, but rather the inevitability of life's problems. I didn't want to talk about success as much as how to weather loss and failure.

But most of all, I intentionally didn't want to give the reader a road map, a how-to, a step-by-step program to achieving all their dreams or whatever. I wanted to leave the advice open-ended, to help the reader ask better questions rather than give them all the answers.

Because ultimately, "giving a fuck" is a question of values. What are you choosing to care about, and what are you choosing to *not* care about? There are no universally right/wrong answers to values. Everyone's will be different. You may value time with your family more than I do. And that's fine. I may value Russian literature or seventies kung fu movies more than you do. And *that's* fine. There's nothing "right" or "wrong" about any of it.

[handwritten annotation: amen]

Therefore, when writing a book about values, it felt important to me to *not* enforce any values onto the reader. The "subtle art" of not giving a fuck is really the art of discovering that it is up to *you* to choose what is worth caring about and what is not. My job as an author is to merely help you discover, acknowledge, and ask these difficult questions for yourself. To push my own values and tell you exactly what to give a fuck about would undermine the power of the message.

In the years since, the book has gone on to become a mega-bestseller, getting translated into more than sixty languages, selling more than ten million copies, and reaching number one in more than a dozen countries. In the intervening years, the most common question I get from readers is, "This is all great and I understand it, but what should I do? Where do I even start?"

Early on, I would privately suggest some exercises to people. "Maybe you should try to write the five things you couldn't live without," I would say. Start there.

Eventually, I was giving out these little exercises enough that I put some of them on my website or sent them out to my email list. People loved them and kept reporting great results.

Over the years, the exercises expanded, multiplied, and were refined. I asked for feedback, created new questions, and shared them again and again. Eventually, I found myself with half a book's worth of questions and journaling prompts—all based on deep, important life questions that few people have ever stopped and taken the time to think about.

This journal is a collection and expansion of those initial exercises. True to the original book, they will not tell you what to value or who to be, but rather they will help you get a clearer sense of what you value and who you wish to be. They are the logical next steps from the questions raised in the book to the questions you should be answering for yourself.

The journal is divided into five parts. The first part consists of a couple exercises I call "The Warm-Up." These are general, abstract questions about what you want in life, what you hope to accomplish before you die, etc. These questions can be fun and useful, but they're mostly designed to get you into the right headspace going into the rest of the journal.

Part 2 is about helping you manage negative emotions. Most of us struggle to figure out what we should give a fuck about because we're too caught up in pain, anger, and sadness. It's only by managing these negative emotions and/or channeling them in a more positive direction that we free ourselves to think about the deeper questions.

Part 3 focuses on choice and responsibility. We all like to delude ourselves into thinking that we didn't choose any of our problems, that they were just thrust upon us by an unfair universe. But the truth is that most of our life is a product of our own choices, and it's only in recognizing those choices—and making better ones!—that we're able to resolve any of our problems.

Once we've chilled the fuck out about our emotions and acknowledged our problems, we then get to the good stuff in part 4: What are you choosing to give a fuck about? What do you wish you gave more of a fuck about? What do you wish you gave less of a fuck about? Are these good fucks to give/not give?

This is the section about values—what we've chosen to care about and whether or not we should consider prioritizing other things in our life higher/lower than they currently are.

These difficult questions then lead us into part 5, which is an elaborate action plan. Through a series of exercises, I will help you take stock of how you're spending your time and if this time spent reflects what you care about (or wish to care about) from part 4. Part 5 will then wrap up with you developing some actionable steps for yourself. It'll be up to you to actually, you know, go do them. Why? Because I don't have a fucking clue who you are or what you do.

Between each part, I've included a series of "interludes"—small sections that complement ideas from the previous section and/or offer small exercises to prepare you for the next section. The back of the journal also has a bunch of empty pages for you to jot down any "Holy Shit!" moments you have along the way, of which I hope there are many.

Enjoy the descent into your own identity. I hope you like what you see. Even if you don't, I'm confident you will come out the other end a better person than you were going in.

Happy fucks-giving,
Mark Manson
September 13, 2021

PART I:
THE WARM-UP

SHUT UP AND BE GRATEFUL

Gratitude is like vitamin D for the soul. A small dose provides an immunity boost to bullshit and helps keep your psychological health strong.

Consciously practicing gratitude periodically is one of the most scientifically supported mental exercises that contributes to happiness and well-being.

Besides, it's nice to take a moment every once in a while and consider what's amazing in your life. So, let's start this party the right way and consider the many things for which we're grateful.

INSTRUCTIONS:

Use this list to write down the many things for which you're grateful. It can be abstract ("I'm grateful for being alive in the twenty-first century.") or specific ("I'm grateful that gas station I stopped at had my favorite energy drink.").

Basically, go gratitude-crazy here. Try to fill these pages up.

EXAMPLES:

- *I'm grateful that I get to travel for my job as much as I do.*
- *I'm grateful that caffeine was discovered in the sixteenth century and is so readily available in the morning.*
- *I'm grateful for my relationship. I'm fortunate to have found such a great person.*

YOUR TURN:

1. Im grateful For ~~Jaeden~~ Pookie for helping me out
2. Im grateful that the Sun shines daily
3. Im grateful for my family that I do have
4. Im grateful for having roofs over my head
5. Im grateful that Im Still breathing
6. Im grateful for anything that comes my way
7. Im grateful for having clothes & shoes
8. Im grateful for all the Kids I/Ive taken care of.
9. Im grateful for waking up everyday &
10. Im grateful for my Sisters not going through the ~~Jmost tramatic~~ issues Ive been through
11. Im grateful for having Food and liquids
12. Im grateful For Friends
13. Im grateful my parent's are still alive 2C me
14. Im grateful for having this Book Rn.

15. _____
16. _____
17. _____
18. _____
19. _____
20. _____
21. _____
22. _____
23. _____
24. _____
25. _____
26. _____
27. _____
28. _____

29. _____

30. _____

31. _____

32. _____

33. _____

34. _____

35. _____

36. _____

37. _____

38. _____

39. _____

40. _____

41. _____

42. _____

43. _____
44. _____
45. _____
46. _____
47. _____
48. _____
49. _____
50. _____
51. _____
52. _____
53. _____
54. _____
55. _____
56. _____

57. _____

58. _____

59. _____

60. _____

61. _____

62. _____

63. _____

64. _____

65. _____

66. _____

67. _____

68. _____

69. _____

70. _____

71. ___
72. ___
73. ___
74. ___
75. ___
76. ___
77. ___
78. ___
79. ___
80. ___
81. ___
82. ___
83. ___
84. ___

Take comfort: no one actually knows what the hell they're doing. Everyone is just working off their current best guess.

YOUR FUCK-IT LIST

Okay, now that we've spewed out all of the things we're grateful for in our lives, let's consider the other side of the coin. Much of "not giving a fuck" is correctly identifying the people and things in your life that are not adding value or helping you as a person . . . and then letting go of them.

Old people create "bucket lists" of things they want to do before they die. We're going to create a "fuck-it list," or things we want to stop giving a fuck about before we die.

Much of this journal will be showing you *how* to stop giving a fuck about them, but for now, let's just get a nice brainstorm out of all of the dumb bullshit holding us back in our lives.

Again, this can be as abstract ("fear of failure") or specific ("when my brother makes fun of my hair") as you want. Whatever it is you want to *stop* caring about, write it down.

EXAMPLES:

- *Saying "yes" too often to things I don't want to do.*
- *The bullshit drama my family starts for no reason.*
- *The anxiety of living up to everyone's expectations.*

YOUR TURN:

1.
2.
3.
4.
5.
6.
7.
8.
9.
10.
11. Fk caring about everyones feelings
12. letting people FK Me over
13. FK letting the Judge Me
14. FK everyones beliefs that they thought they had before Me

15. _____
16. _____
17. _____
18. _____
19. _____
20. _____
21. _____
22. _____
23. _____
24. _____
25. _____
26. _____
27. _____
28. _____
29. _____

30. _____
31. _____
32. _____
33. _____
34. _____
35. _____
36. _____
37. _____
38. _____
39. _____
40. _____
41. _____
42. _____
43. _____
44. _____

45. _____
46. _____
47. _____
48. _____
49. _____
50. _____
51. _____
52. _____
53. _____
54. _____
55. _____
56. _____
57. _____
58. _____
59. _____

60. _____

61. _____

62. _____

63. _____

64. _____

65. _____

66. _____

67. _____

68. _____

69. _____

70. _____

With these two exercises under our belts, now we have a rough idea of both *what we want to add* to our lives and *what we want to remove* from our lives. The rest of this journal will provide exercises and processes to help you do both of these things.

To get started, we will address what stops most people before they even get started: handling their negative emotions.

Self-awareness is like an onion. There are multiple layers to it, and the more you peel them back the more likely you're going to start crying at inappropriate times.

PART II:
MANAGING NEGATIVE EMOTIONS

CUT THE EMOTIONAL CRAP

Emotions are these things that . . . happen. They dominate your existence for a while and then they're gone. And then, just when you think you're free, another emotion comes along and hijacks your shit all over again. *all dun bro*

Experiencing an intense emotion is kind of like going through high school: When you're in it, nothing feels more important. But when it's over, you can only laugh at all of the dumb things you thought were important.

Over the years, I've made a regular habit of criticizing our overreliance on our emotions. I've written articles with titles like "Fuck Your Feelings" and "Happiness Is Not Enough" and compared my readers' temper tantrums to a dog shitting on a carpet. (Sorry about that, by the way.) But the truth is, emotions *do matter*. They are incredibly important. They're just not important in the ways we think they are.

Emotions serve an important purpose: They are your brain's way of telling you something good or bad is happening in your life. They provide feedback to help you process reality.

But that's about it. They're not cosmic messages from the universe telling you to go back to school. They are not fate trying to teach you a lesson. No wings of destiny carrying you away from your relationship here; that's all shit made up in your head to justify what you already feel. Your emotions are simply feedback mechanisms designed to let you know whether things are going well or not. Nothing more. Nothing less.

The thing that messes people up is that they let their emotions inform life decisions—big and small—because they feel that their emotions do hold this extremely high level of importance, which they don't. People mistake their emotions *as their purpose* instead of using their emotions to *find their sense of purpose*.

Just think back to some of the stupidest decisions you've ever made. Chances are most of those decisions were motivated by you being an emotional time bomb. Maybe you were angry and in a fit of rage, smashed your keyboard against your desk, causing you to get fired. Maybe you were so sad from your breakup that you drank yourself into a stupor, blacked out, drove home, and woke up in a jail cell. Maybe you were so anxious that you passed on a huge career opportunity that you've always wanted.

Whatever it is, we've all been there. Our emotions hijack our sense of reality, and suddenly something that would be a good decision on any other day feels like a horribly laborious, bad decision. Or what is obviously a terrible idea draws us in with an irresistible force, until we wake up in a pool of our own vomit wondering what happened.

Our emotions have a knack for derailing our decision-making. This means that when you base your life on your emotions, you're constantly up and down, running around in circles, contradicting yourself, changing your mind, forgetting what you've said and done. All in an effort to find and maintain the next emotional high. That's no way to live.

This part of the journal is designed to help you identify the purpose of any emotion you might be struggling with. The exercises in this section enable you to look at the "signals" you receive from your brain more objectively in order to know what to do with the feedback once you've felt it.

This is a useful skill to hone because while receiving signals is an important part of navigating the world and your place in it, what you do with that information is an entirely different matter. As you will learn by completing this section of the journal, interpretations of and reactions to emotions are far more important than the emotions themselves.

There's no such thing as a good or bad emotion, only good or bad reactions to emotions.

How Are You Feeling?

What emotion are you currently struggling with? What happened? Describe the situation and how you've reacted to it.

EXAMPLE:

I am so angry. Jason completely broke my trust the other day. I asked him months ago if he could help me organize an event and he said yes. Then, out of nowhere, weeks before the event, he tells me he's not sure anymore. It's like, dude, you fucking committed to this. I was depending on you. I spent thousands of dollars and scheduled much of that week based on your commitment. Now, I'm scrambling to do damage control. And even worse, I'm pretty sure a guy I thought was my friend is a total asshole. Either that or he's secretly jealous or something and trying to sabotage my shit. What the fuck!

YOUR TURN:

I am frustrated at the Family Fr! they never listen, I always help them wen they need it the most! I depended on them for the security and cant get that huh. I shut them out to avoid conflict Fr. yall might have sacrificed alot for me! but mine in return wasnt enaff for yall, but thats ok bc one day youll understand how I truly felt. I always wanted to be I dont understand how you cant c wats going on with me I vs I you. I want different outcomes, different similar things. - Desperate things -

Emotions are part of the equation of our lives, but not the *entire* equation.

I dont wanna be here fr! silence is heaven for me unlike most. It Doesn't seem to b real most of the time Doesnt equal the pain I get constantly from everything Day by Day it gets worse uk! Shutting people out is what we do! tell me what im supposed to Do? Fk everyone at this point, ik my worth if i really think about it. things I wanna acclompish will be my goal for now on tbh! Its pretty depressing on a lotta shit i dont need.
i want a New change!!!

How did you react to the emotion? Did you express it? If so, how? If not, why not?

EXAMPLE:

If I'm being honest, I didn't express it. Inside, I freaked out, but I didn't want to start a fight. I just figured, All right, if this is the kind of friend and colleague you are, good to know. Now I know not to ever work with him again. Since then, I've been passive-aggressive. I haven't returned most of his texts. I've ignored a couple emails. Last time he was in town, I didn't invite him out or anything. I know I should probably say something. But seriously, fuck him.

YOUR TURN:

despite everything i expressed litterally all inside and never out loud. i barely like anything to do with him. being stranded in your own thoughts aint as easy as they say. beleiving he can change is crazy to the-T. FK him and his non holy ass lmao I am and will carry on his weight as long as he carry mine periodt but atp fuck it.

Often our problem is not the emotion itself, but rather how we respond to the emotion. Sometimes we judge the emotion and try to bury it because we don't see it as acceptable.

What about you? Have you been judging the emotion in an unhelpful way? If so, how?

Overall, do you think you've responded to the emotion in a healthy way or unhealthy way?

EXAMPLE:

I've always had trouble confronting people, especially when it feels like they've been disrespectful toward me. I just bury it and hold on to the resentment for a long time. I know that's not healthy, but I suppose somewhere deep down I feel like it's not acceptable to be angry at people. I have trouble expressing my anger in general. I'm always the calm, cool, collected guy who is really chill and nothing ever bothers me. That's great. But when something does actually bother me, I need to be able to speak up.

YOUR TURN:

me having trouble with confronting saying out loud, or even eye contact disturbs my ass to the core ideky. I keep my mouth shut so they cant judge, but is that ok? normal? who knows really. defining the trust & communication is difficult. will I forgive him, maybe, I need to come out & say what I need to say but after all of this im scared to why? because, i hold on to broken things that cant be fixed and they need 2.

Negative emotions are a call to action. They are nature's preferred agent to inspire change.

Cognitive Distortions

Cognitive distortions are a set of automatic thought patterns that are inaccurate and reinforce our emotions. These automatic negative thoughts "distort" our thinking by leading us to believe something that is both unhelpful and likely untrue.

Psychiatrist and researcher Aaron Beck is credited with first proposing the theory behind cognitive distortions in the 1970s; his student David Burns is credited with popularizing the common names of these distortions in the 1980s.

Have a look at these twelve cognitive distortions and see if you can recognize any of the thought patterns as you deal with your current emotional situation.

ALL-OR-NOTHING THINKING

This is the assumption that your issues are black and white and only two explanations for something exist. For example, someone is either a wonderful friend or a piece of shit. A work project is either brilliant or unbelievably stupid. You assume people either love you and are obsessed with you or hate you and wish you were dead.

BLAMING OTHERS

Holding other people accountable for a shitty situation is often easier than taking responsibility yourself. In my example, blaming Jason for abandoning the event is easier than realizing that there were other ways I could have gotten him to guarantee his commitment (e.g., asking him to sign a contract) and/or I could have lined up someone else to help as a backup.

CATASTROPHIZING

Focusing on the worst, most unpleasant possible outcome to a relatively small issue or event is unhelpful and really melodramatic. Things don't always have to feel like the end of the world—leave that feeling for the doomsayers.

EMOTIONAL REASONING

Just because you feel it, doesn't make it true. It's easy to read emotions as truth in the heat of the moment, but emotions are not reliable indicators of reality. Even if you strongly feel your colleague is out to get you, not only is that probably not true, but your colleague probably isn't even thinking that much about you—you are thinking about you.

FORTUNE-TELLING

If there's one thing you can be certain of, it's that you can be certain of nothing. Yet, we still all love to play the role of Nostradamus and assume we know *exactly* what is going to happen, I.e., just because you *feel* embarrassed doesn't mean your career is ruined.

LABELING

"I made a mistake on the data sheet; therefore, I am a moron." Labeling is where a person makes big judgments about someone's personal character based on small experiences. You and I do this all the time when we're driving in traffic—that guy who cut us off is not actually a horribly selfish human being. The woman who ran the red light is not clueless or deranged. And the person who stole your parking spot is not going to hell . . . as much as you'd like them to.

MAGNIFYING THE NEGATIVE

Your emotions often cause you to look at a situation with tunnel vision. When you magnify the negative you tend to ignore anything positive that might have happened . . . which might actually make you feel less miserable about the situation.

MINIMIZING THE POSITIVE

To allow negativity to live and breathe even more freely, some people actively quash the value or importance of the positive aspects of a situation. When we downplay our accomplishments and insist that anyone could have done what we did, we are downplaying the positive.

MIND READING

Just like fortune-telling, mind reading makes dramatic predictions about reality without much evidence. But whereas we use fortune-telling in an attempt to predict the future based on our emotions, we use mind reading in an attempt to assume we know what someone else is thinking/feeling based on our own emotions. For example, if I assume Jason secretly hates me and is trying to sabotage my event, that would be mind reading.

OVERGENERALIZATION

Applying blanket assumptions to your situation based on isolated past experiences and little evidence leads to broad and unrealistic conclusions. Stereotypes about various kinds of people are the most common (and socially destructive) form of overgeneralization. But we do this about pretty much anything. Like when couples argue and say things like, "You *always* do this" or "You *only* care about that." Yeah, no bueno . . .

SELF-BLAMING

Self-blaming is the belief that everything is your own fault, that if anything bad happens to you, it's because you're an idiot or evil or a total doofus. Self-blaming is really just a form of self-absorption—it's usually an emotionally-driven attempt to constantly garner sympathy. And it's not really helpful for anyone.

"SHOULD" STATEMENTS

If you think you or someone else *should* have done something and there's little wiggle room for alternatives of how things could have played out, then you are setting unfair rules and expectations on yourself or other people. This sort of distortion leads to feelings of guilt and anger.

Okay, now that we've reviewed cognitive distortions, which ones do you think apply to your situation?

For example, in my situation, I am totally blaming Jason even though there are things I could have done to prevent the situation.

I'm labelling him because I'm basically assuming he's an untrustworthy piece of shit. I'm catastrophizing because, let's be honest, things will be fine. And finally, I'm mind reading by assuming his intentions without even talking to him!

All-or-Nothing Thinking	Fortune-Telling	Minimizing the Positive
Blaming Others (circled)	**Labeling** (circled)	Overgeneralization
Catastrophizing (circled)	Magnifying the Negative	Self-Blaming
Emotional Reasoning	**Mind Reading** (circled)	"Should" Statements

YOUR TURN:

All-or-Nothing Thinking	Fortune-Telling	Minimizing the Positive
All-or-Nothing Thinking (circled)	Fortune-Telling	Minimizing the Positive
Blaming Others	**Labeling** (circled)	**Overgeneralization** (circled)
Catastrophizing	**Magnifying the Negative** (circled)	Self-Blaming
Emotional Reasoning (circled)	Mind Reading	**"Should" Statements** (circled)

Now, let's try to describe your situation again, this time without succumbing to cognitive distortions.

EXAMPLE:

Jason totally blindsided me by bailing on the event he promised to help with. But to be honest, I don't know what's going on in his life. Maybe it's justified. Maybe it's not. It's deeply disappointing, and I am angry at him. But I can find somebody else, and with a little extra work, things will be fine.

YOUR TURN:

ima over come everything and have the expections i really need day by Day ima have me back And do wat I do most! he'll never understand It. If i can make or help him then Fuck yeah. I promised myself to keep myself outta these situations but ill be fine Really. Ill prove it to most I promise.

The desire for a positive experience is itself a negative experience. And, paradoxically, the acceptance of one's negative experience is itself a positive experience.

Emotions are neutral. Each emotion can be both healthy or unhealthy depending *on our reactions to that emotion.*

Unhealthy reactions are dishonest, ambiguous, destructive, pointless, or violent.

Healthy reactions are honest, transparent, constructive, educational, and growth-oriented.

Here are some examples of how each emotion can be reacted to in both unhealthy and healthy ways.

ANGER
- Destructive when directed to hurt yourself or others
- Useful when correcting injustices and/or protecting yourself or others

FEAR
- Frustrating when it prevents you from pursuing your dreams
- Very helpful when being chased by an angry tiger

JOY
- Corrosive when used to justify a sense of superiority over others
- Wonderful when shared because something good happens

SADNESS
- Damaging when it prevents you from living a normal life
- Moving when it helps you honor the memory of what you have lost

SHAME
- Harmful when it causes you to judge and hate yourself unnecessarily
- Favorable when preventing you from doing something inappropriate

CURIOSITY

- Dangerous when it inspires you to gargle a glass of bleach . . . you know, for science
- Amazing when it helps you explore this incredible world and life

Now, returning to your situation again, what are the healthy and unhealthy forms of the emotion in your situation?

EXAMPLE:

The unhealthy way of dealing with my anger toward Jason would be to bury it or let it prevent me from trusting others again. It'd also be unhealthy if I allowed my anger to justify me being shitty to him in return. The healthy way to deal with the anger is to talk to him about it, tell him how I feel, and ask him what's going on. If he responds with honesty and accountability, then I will be able to live with that. If he doesn't, then I know that I've lost a friend.

YOUR TURN:

I can change by asserting myself in positive situations instead of negative
actually sit down and listen
ima not let them fk me over
its not really my plan to destroy my love for someone

Despite what every cliche says, we shouldn't necessarily trust our own emotions. In fact, we should make a habit of questioning them.

If reactions to emotions are more important than the emotions themselves, then we must judge people (and ourselves) by actions, not emotions.

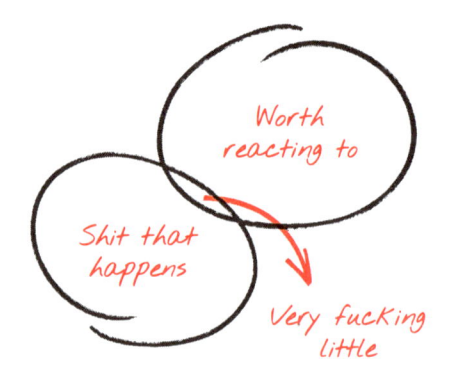

Worth reacting to

Shit that happens

Very fucking little

We often judge ourselves (and others) for our emotions, but this is usually unfair because we're not in control of the emotions we experience. If there's one thing you take away from this part of the journal, it's this: *there's no such thing as a bad emotion—there are only bad reactions to emotions.*

Emotions are a normal and an unavoidable part of life. There is nothing wrong or shameful about feeling any emotion. However, wallowing in emotions is a choice. Succumbing to our emotions is a choice. Using an emotion as an excuse to throw a temper tantrum is a choice.

It's better to judge people based on how people *choose to act* on their emotions—on how well they are able to feel emotions, recognize them, and then move on.

As a final exercise, I want you to return to your situation one last time, this time asking yourself, "What is a healthy reaction to this upsetting situation?" What is a reaction that minimizes cognitive distortions; that produces better, healthier outcomes for everyone involved; and that promotes transparency and honesty?

EXAMPLE:

It's clear to me that the best thing I can do in my situation is simply talk to Jason and try to understand why he let me down like this. Similarly, I need to tell him how angry and disappointed I am, rather than keeping it in and letting it fester into resentment and judgment. I know he's not a bad guy.

Who knows what is going on in his life? I should
probably try to find out. I should also probably sit
down and try to figure out what I can do in the
future to prevent this from happening again—keeping
my personal life and business life separate may be
a good start. Using a contract next time might be
good as well.

YOUR TURN:

the best thing I've done is keep my
composure, deepest thing I treasured
was people comfronting me about how
they see me. the real me :), shit that
pops up pop out hits different.
healthy relationship to me is easy
simple and something I cherish
more everyday.

INTERLUDE:
FUCK HAPPINESS

Five Things That Prevent Happiness:

1. Worrying about happiness
2. Worrying that you're worrying about happiness
3. Worrying that you worry too much
4. Taxes
5. Worrying about taxes

Ah, the pinnacle of the human experience, the obsession and desire of every living person: happiness.

We like to think that happiness is the holy grail of emotions—the place we'd like to find, inhabit, and never leave.

But I'd like to leave you with another thought: Happiness is not an emotion to be found. Happiness is the lack of other emotions.

If emotions are feedback mechanisms from your body telling your mind that something needs to change, then happiness is the lack of that feedback—it's the moment where nothing needs to change. Where everything is wonderful as it is.

Therefore, happiness is not created by finding something more and pursuing something outside of ourselves. Rather, happiness is found by letting go and focusing on less.

PART III:
BETTER PROBLEMS

DON'T HOPE FOR A LIFE WITHOUT PROBLEMS

We all salivate at the thought of a problem-free life full of everlasting joy and happiness, but that's the stuff terrible dreams are made of.

Here's a hard truth to accept: Life's problems are unavoidable. They never stop being thrown at you. In fact, it's only by trying to dodge the endless series of problems coming your way that you make them so much worse.

Solving problems gives us a sense of purpose. Therefore, in order to be satisfied with ourselves, we *need* problems to solve. This means that the solution to one problem should always be the creation of the next problem. The trick is to make sure you are creating better problems each time you solve a problem. It's exchanging all your problems for upgraded problems.

No one should be trying for a life without struggle: that's impossible. Instead, we should simply be looking to struggle for better reasons. A good life means having good problems. We don't ever completely rid ourselves of problems; rather, we simply improve upon them. A homeless man has money problems. Warren Buffett has money problems. But we'd all much rather have Warren Buffett's money problems than the homeless man's.

Put another way, progress is in the improvement of problems.

In this part of the journal, you will be looking at the problems in your life and asking yourself how you can improve upon them. Instead of looking to rid yourself of the problems or thinking positively about your problems, you'll simply ask yourself, *What is the better problem to have here?*

Let's get to it.

What's Your Problem?

Think about a problem you're struggling with in your life. Describe the situation.

EXAMPLE:

My partner is upset because we aren't spending enough time together and she wants me to be more proactive in organizing quality time. It's difficult for me to remember to think about these sorts of things. I actually didn't even realize it was a problem until she lost it at me for not being around enough.

YOUR TURN:

problems-
weight
Mental
health
love
Commenment
Freedom From peope
being who i really wanna be
Realizing everyone aint for Me

What's Your Problem?

The first step to addressing any problem is to determine what aspects of the problem we can control and what aspects we can't control. So much of the time, we get worked up and try to change things that are outside of our control. Similarly, we complain and deflect responsibility for the things we *can* control. Until we can straighten these two categories out, we won't get anywhere.

WHAT YOU CAN *NEVER* CHANGE:

- The past
- The world
- Other people

WHAT YOU CAN *ALWAYS* CHANGE:

- Your attitude
- Your assumptions
- Your behavior

Write down the aspects of your problem that are *out of your control* and the aspects of your problem that are *within your control.*

EXAMPLE:

I can't control how my partner feels. I also can't control that she seems to need more time together than I do to be satisfied in the relationship. What I can control is how often I'm around and, more importantly, how I communicate my availability to her. Often I'm not around not because I don't want to be, but because I have so many other obligations.

YOUR TURN:

whats out of control -
I cant control other people around me that do hard drugs, I'll relapse quick... my family is also ~~something~~ something I cant control and mainly peoples opinions, their tourture sometimes, but you cant control non of it, cant change the past? so why does it haunt me the most. I would change my attitude, my ANGER! is most controlling over me! I can <u>help</u> change things cant make them change.
I do have many many more out comes and problems to go but I'll get there for sure ♡

The vast majority of problems don't just occur out of nowhere. We have made various choices that have led to the problem, so we are partially responsible for the problem. This sense of responsibility is actually empowering because it enables us to change our choices in the future. Now, let's look at the choices you've made in the past that have led to your problem.

EXAMPLE:

I chose to prioritize my work over my relationship because I felt it was more important for me at the time. I chose to work late and on weekends. I chose to go to bed early because I was exhausted. I chose to ignore my partner a number of times.

YOUR TURN:

I chose to stay quiet while I needed to say sum.

I chose to keep my body still when pain endures.

I chose to smoke then to get clean completly.

I chose Drugs period over my family.

I chose to not get the correct attention.

I Didnt want to change at First!

I chose friends that weren't my friends.

True happiness occurs only when you find problems you enjoy having and enjoy solving.

So enjoy what
you can enjoy ♡

Are you satisfied with those choices? Would you go back and change them? Keep in mind that no is always an acceptable answer here—if that's the case, then this is the problem you chose!

EXAMPLE:

I don't regret prioritizing my work, but I certainly ignored how it would affect my relationship, which was definitely a mistake. I don't want to work this much forever, and I do want to prioritize my relationship higher in the future. I can work to communicate this better.

YOUR TURN:

I wanna change.

I wanna Do Better.

I Dont wanna fail.

I will Succeed In life.

Different Days Different Days.

I wanna create what I couldnt already.

I want a different Body.

I will correct Myself For Me

Communicate More

Be more Free Will. For Me ♡

Now that you've decided what choices you'd like to change, it's time to come up with a list of potential actions that will enact those new choices.

EXAMPLES:

- *I can designate Wednesday nights as date night.*
- *I can buy flowers or her favorite gelato on my way home to show her I care, even if I'm not around.*
- *I can make sure we spend weekend mornings together like we used to.*

YOUR TURN:

have better rutines.
focus more on future schooling or sooner
I can make more time for me & not others
I will show more appriecation towards things
Never compeare myself to others
I can change my point of veiw on things & people
I can concure more things if Im constantly proceeding on mature things

Great! Obviously, go do this stuff. But, let's prevent ourselves from having to deal with this mess again. Ask yourself, what are the potential problems that will arise from these new choices? Are these better problems? If not, then you might want to go back a couple steps and re-evaluate your decisions again!

EXAMPLES:

- I'll have to figure out what to do on date nights more often.
- My commute home will be longer if I stop to buy things for her.
- I'll have to put in the effort to be more focused and present with her.

YOUR TURN:

So far nothing Rn cuz Im handling it more better then b4 so thats something taking it day by day ♡ i'll never compare myself to others because Ik what I actually can do.

~~████████████████~~ I wanna b more independent and more stable tbh I need to put more energy in things and dont let shit hold me back.

Generally, when shit blows up in our life, our first reaction is to whine and moan and say, "Why is this happening to me?"

But instead, let's try asking, "What can I learn from this?"

Because it's impossible to regret something that has ultimately benefited you. Learning from our bad choices can potentially turn them into good choices.

So, what have you learned from this problem?

EXAMPLE:

I definitely took my relationship for granted. I didn't realize how much work is necessary to keep us both happy, even three or four years into it. I learned to communicate my priorities to her better. I also learned that little gestures and small amounts of effort can go a long way. I always assumed that coming home for lunch or buying her a small gift was so tiny that it was pointless, but now I'm realizing that those little things can mean a lot.

YOUR TURN:

I've learned that I can choose my own path but I gotta b smarter! to create the dreams I've built! I need to communicate more better shit that I witnessed and know now is shit I learned from not doing etc. different days different hrs prove I can start my career be more considerate.

INTERLUDE:
SACRIFICE IS THE SECRET

As you move through life, upgrading from one problem to a slightly better problem to a slightly better problem than that, you will begin to notice something: giving up stuff feels kind of good.

See, when we're young and immature, we like to entertain this idea that we can have everything, we can do everything, we can be everything. Our concept of "improvement" is getting more for less.

But what we realize as we get older and begin to improve from problem to problem is that when we find the problems we like, we're happy to give up things. We're happy to make sacrifices. We like giving up part of our weekends to make our relationships better. We like making the sacrifice at work to improve team morale. We like helping out others in need.

And not only do we like these things, but they become the most valuable things. Sacrifice is not the antithesis of a satisfied and fulfilled life. Sacrifice is a satisfied and fulfilled life.

PART IV:
GIVING FEWER FUCKS

WHO YOU ARE IS DEFINED BY YOUR VALUES

Every moment of every day, whether you realize it or not, you are deciding how to spend your time, what to pay attention to, where to direct your energy.

Right now, you are choosing to use this journal. Fuck yeah! There are an infinite number of things you could be doing instead, but right now, you are choosing to be here with this journal. Maybe in a second, someone will text you and you'll put the journal down. Maybe you'll decide to watch a movie. Maybe you'll realize you really need to pee.

When those things happen, you are making a simple, value-based decision: your phone (or your toilet) is more valuable to you than using the journal at that moment. Your behavior follows that valuation accordingly.

Our values are constantly reflected in the way we choose to behave. The things we choose to prioritize. This is critically important—because we all have a few things that we think and say we value, but we never back them up with our actions. In fact, we're *often* operating at a level of disconnect between what we say we value and what we actually spend our time doing.

I mean, I can tell people (and myself) until I'm blue in the face that I care about climate change or the dangers of social media, but if I spend my days driving around in a gas-guzzling SUV and constantly refreshing my newsfeed, then my behaviors, my actions, tell a different story. Just like hips, actions don't lie. You might believe you want to get that job, but when push comes to shove, you'll always be kind of relieved that no one called you back so you can retreat into video games again.

Unfortunately, it's usually only when we experience intense pain or disruptions to our lives that we're actually willing to look at our values and question why they seem to be failing us. That's when we're able to clearly identify the disconnects between what we say and believe and what we actually *do*.

When we are disconnected from our values—e.g., prioritizing video games but believing we value ambition and hard work—our beliefs and ideas get separated from our actions and emotions. Trying to bridge these disconnects leads us to becoming delusional, about both ourselves and the world. This is where things start to deteriorate. This is where this journal comes in.

By using this part of the journal, you will begin to develop a clear understanding of the values and behaviors you actually want to adopt, of the identities you want to shed or step into, as well as the life you want for yourself. By the time you're done here, you should have a clear sense of who you are and how you need to behave to align yourself to that vision.

Let's Get Started . . .

Before you use this section to work through an issue you're having, I'd like you to list your highest values so it's always here for you to come back to when you are completing a set of questions. Personal values should be used as measuring sticks by which we determine what is a successful and meaningful life. So the point is to nail down some good ones. By articulating your values upfront, you'll be in a better position to identify patterns of behavior that are contradicting the awesome person you're trying to uncover.

GOOD VALUES ARE

- reality-based,
- constructive, and
- controllable.

BAD VALUES ARE

- emotion-based,
- destructive, and
- uncontrollable.

Good values tend to be things that we can control, that help ourselves and others, and that are accurate reflections of reality. Valuing my family is good and healthy. Valuing the Spaghetti Monster and attempting to murder my family in ritual sacrifice is an example of a bad value.

Some examples of good, healthy values: honesty, building something new, vulnerability, standing up for oneself, standing up for others, self-respect, curiosity, charity, humility, and creativity.

Conversely, bad values tend to be outside of our control, are destructive to ourselves and others, and are largely based on our own impulses and not on reality.

Some examples of bad, unhealthy values: dominating others through manipulation or violence, fucking more men/women, feeling good all the time, always being the center of attention, not being alone, being liked by everybody, being rich for the sake of being rich, and sacrificing small animals to the pagan gods.

Think about what is important to you in your life and what kind of person you are. What are your highest values? List out at least ten.

EXAMPLES:

- Honesty
- Creativity
- Family
- Stability
- Health
- Reputation

Tip: *If knowing what you value seems daunting to you, simply ask yourself what problems you enjoy solving that most other people don't. That is what you value. If you are choosing the right problems, you are choosing the right values.*

YOUR TURN:

Family in general

breathing eryday

being able to have a roof over my head

HAving Jaden she my ride or die rn I aint shit without her!

Creativity mostly from mom

Ima humble person but dont take my ass for granted tho.

Now that you've got your list, you can use this section every time you feel unbalanced or disconnected in your life. Working through what's going on and cross-checking against what you believe you value will make it clear whether or not you're really being true to yourself.

Happiness is not something outside of ourselves, it's merely a choice— a choice based on what we choose to value and find important in each moment.

Conflicting Values

Generally, the most difficult moments in our lives occur when we have two conflicting values. We want to excel at work, but we also want to be home for our kids. We want to spend more time with our friends, but we also don't want to abandon our partner. We don't want to pay our taxes, but we also don't want to go to jail for tax evasion. Life is full of these sorts of dilemmas.

When these conflicts happen between two healthy values (i.e., focusing more at work *and* spending more time with the kids), then it becomes a question of priorities and time management.

But often a good value is conflicting with a bad value (i.e., taking care of your health versus going on another all-night bender with your friends). It's these situations that we must look at closely, identify the unhealthy values and what's underpinning them, and then try to alter how much we give a fuck about them.

So, what disruption or conflict are you experiencing in your life that has led you to question your values right now? Describe the situation.

EXAMPLE:

I've always been so close with my family, but lately I feel like no one really cares about me. No one cares about what I'm doing or going through. They used to look after me a lot more, and I don't know what happened. I feel like I should just start giving them less attention.

YOUR TURN:

For starters I put everyone first! apparently but thats ok b/c we already cut hella ppl off! etc. I try and stay calm most of the time & dont say nun but damn the shit irritating uk!

My distruption is honestly me $. Its sad but we come along way fr!

My priorites rn is sum shit could be better but we making it happen fr. and I'm loving every inch of it.

If you're not satisfied with the problems you currently face in your life, then take a long, hard look at the values that put the problems there. Perhaps it's time to change your priorities.

Change is for good?

Me Changing is gonna take
Alot
　But
　　I
　　　Can
　　　　Do
　　　　　It
　　　　　　!!
　　　　　　for
　　　　　　　sure
　　　　　　　　!!!
different life style !!
different ppl !!
new Beginings / new start
　　TAKE It BABY girl
　　　You deserve it.

How have your actions reflected your personal values? It's easy to say we value something, but if we're never actually *doing* it, then how much do we really value it?

EXAMPLE:

I call my mom once a week to see how she's doing. It used to be a few times a week, but I'm so busy now. My sister and I try to catch up once a month, but it's been two months now. I do always remember birthdays, and I try not to miss family events, but it's been difficult since COVID. We all stopped getting together, and now I barely see anyone.

YOUR TURN:

I use to connect with people but not as much bc I see how everyone moves now & I like it. the more I say. Fk It - the more I can do Me and Its Sad.
they reflected pretty much on everybody FR. it also depends on if I FW them. I try to fix It but that never works either.

If you are struggling to match your actions against your values, what are you prioritizing instead? What do your actions actually say? What are you really valuing?

EXAMPLE:

I am spending a lot of time on my own for no particular reason. Sometimes when Dad calls, I'm busy and then I just forget to call back. I actually used to go over to my parents' place every Sunday for dinner, but the last few times I've chosen to go out with friends so I guess my actions are saying that I value my friends over my family.

YOUR TURN:

ion value much b/c ive never had much. and I do be condridicting myself sometimes but mostly for a good cause.

I technically prioritize the lil family moments i can get before they actually gone.
i value my friends more b/c they judge me in a way most Dont so ofc i go them over family. ♡
Sadly no- b/c they shoulda done it first.

i gotta change for myself rr if i dont ima loose my baby sisters from myself which i cant have honestly.

What influences or actions can you *remove* from your life to allow you to better live out your values?

EXAMPLE:

I could probably stop seeing my friends so much. I love them, but I shouldn't keep prioritizing them over my family. I also drink too much with them, and sometimes I'm just way too hungover to do anything with my family.

YOUR TURN:

things I can remove-

1. Anger constantly
2. taking things not seriously
3. living situation
4. family that don't "Gaf"
5. attitude torwards my real dad 19!
6. Stop prioritizing my friends more than my damn self.

Focus on what you can control. Fuck the rest.

Remember, regardless of what you think or feel or wish to be true, true values are reflected in your choices and actions.

Now, look back on your answers and be truthful with yourself. Are these values serving you? Or do you need to look at adopting better values? Reflect here and go back to the beginning of the section to add and/or subtract values if you need to.

I wouldnt say serving me but I feel like if I try harder, or enuff I would achieve anything I put my mind to you know. my values arent even that pricy or volumed! such as every one who has everything gets greedy on what they need ya know! I will forever cherish them.

To replace your old, faulty values with new, healthy values, you need to understand the narratives around your experiences.

Choosing better values is about liberating ourselves from unhealthy ideas and inviting the right kinds of insecurities into our lives.

For example, if you're ashamed of wearing the wrong shoes around your coworkers, then that signals that your values are faulty—that you're more concerned with appearances and the approval of those around you rather than respecting yourself and your own tastes.

Describe a situation where you think replacing a faulty value with a healthier value might have improved your experience.

I care so much on how people see me in general, my weight is a heavy thing on my shoulders I try to b humble for me but it aint always as it seems fr! I do respect myself more now then before but there are them days ♡ yk! I value how people do share sum type of support but wen I give my effort time place thoughts you know I wont get it back so thats a fail automatically.

Other then Baby booh Jaden ♡

There's no such thing as a "bad experience," only an experience that we fail to utilize.

We are all choosing what to give a fuck about in every moment, whether we realize it or not. If you're not asking yourself the important question of what to give a fuck about, then the forces around you will decide your values for you.

Our values determine the nature of our problems, and the nature of our problems determines the quality of our lives. Good values equal a good life.

But how do we change our values?

By changing ourselfs ♡

INTERLUDE:
KNOWING VS DOING

While your values determine your behavior—new behavior determines new values. It's not enough to simply sit here and think about what you wish to value. As my friend Derek Sivers says, "If change was as simple as knowing information, then we'd all be millionaires with six-pack abs."

Take a moment and ask yourself, what are the things in your life that you want to do and know how to do, yet you still don't do them?

I wanna do like photography still or fashion !! maybe my nursing but my heart way to big for that. I want to achieve in anything I could do Fr!

As this list proves, simply valuing something is not enough to make you do it.

Values mean nothing without action. Therefore, the final part of this journal will guide you through setting yourself up for new actions and behaviors.

PART V:
FIND GREATER PURPOSE

The rare people who do become truly exceptional at something do so not because they believe they're exceptional. On the contrary, they become amazing because they're obsessed with improvement.

HOW TO BUILD A BETTER LIFE

Let's start things off here with a simple question: Are you living the life you want to live?

If the answer isn't an immediate and enthusiastic, "Fuck yes," then something's wrong.

This part of the journal is designed to help you answer this question and take action to changing your life for the better. This may seem a little daunting, but we'll break it down into manageable chunks. You'll then be able to refer back to these steps and act on them over the coming months and years. This can be an annual process—every year we need to re-evaluate where we are and where we're going.

This system is an adaptation of a similar exercise a good friend of mine has done every year for well over a decade. I've modified it with some other goal-setting techniques I've come across over the years so you may recognize parts of it. It's not revolutionary by any means. But it works. And that's what's important.

Changes are coming your way quicker than you think & Baby Girl a luv yourself

The Foundation for a Better Life

Before we dive headfirst into creating an action plan, I want you to consider what would make you a happier, more fulfilled person. What would make your life better than it is right now?

Is it more money? More sex? More love, adoration, and respect from your family, friends, and peers? Exploring more and trying "new things"? Finding more meaningful work?

Is it all of those things?

Whatever it is you think will make you a happier person, I'm willing to bet it falls into one or more of the following categories: freedom (financial or otherwise), relationships, or health. That's because these are the three major components of happiness. And if you seriously lack one or more of these in your life, it's virtually impossible to feel fulfilled.

All growth requires loss. A loss of your old values, your old behaviors, your old loves, your old identity. Therefore, growth sometimes has a component of grief to it. *Amen Sista*

FREEDOM

If you think you lack freedom and feel like you have little control over how you spend your time, then you're not going to feel very content most days.

This is why people with high-paying jobs who work more than eighty hours a week are often miserable. Sure they have money, but they have no freedom, no sense of control over how they spend their time. The cliche says that money can't buy happiness. And that's true. But when used correctly, money can buy you freedom. When used incorrectly, money can actually make you less free.

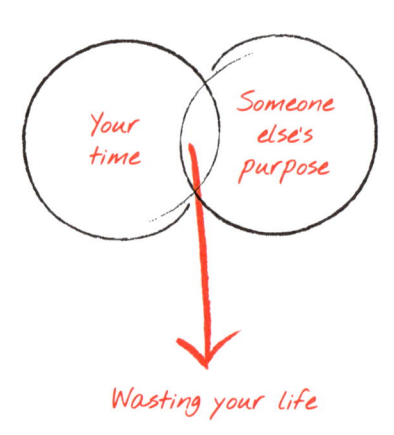

Your time ∩ Someone else's purpose → Wasting your life

Conversely, this is why people who earn more modest incomes but have more flexibility in their jobs are often happier than those who don't. To an extent, the way you make your money is more important than how much money you make.

RELATIONSHIPS Bummer tbh

We've heard too many stories about the three-times-divorced celebrity who tears up in an interview and says he'd give away his fortune for just one good relationship and children who actually talk to him.

In all of the data on happiness and life satisfaction, the quality of our relationships has the greatest impact on the quality of our lives. The better our relationships, the happier and more satisfied we are. The worse our relationships, well . . . the more of a dumpster fire we find ourselves in.

HEALTH Sad n sorry

Of course, all the freedom and fulfilling relationships in the world don't mean much if you don't have your health. Here's another cliche example: Go down to the cancer ward at your local hospital and ask someone on their deathbed if they'd rather have a zillion dollars or not have cancer anymore. Be prepared for some serious glares and maybe a bedpan or two thrown in your direction.

HAPPINESS TRIANGLE

We've all heard these cliched parables repeatedly throughout our lives, but many of us don't catch on to see that it's not just one of these things that makes us happy. You need some degree of all three. To feel a sense of contentment and happiness in your life, at least some of the time, freedom, fulfilling relationships, and your health are paramount.

The point of all this is that I want you to keep these three areas in mind when going through this section. You may find that you have solid relationships and that you're young and healthy, but what's really draining your enjoyment of life is a lack of freedom because of your job. That's good to know. Work on that. But not at the expense of your relationships and health.

The beauty of this "happiness triangle" is that getting one of these areas of your life in order can create a positive feedback loop with the others. Finding a job or starting a business that doesn't strap you to a desk against your will for fifty weeks out of the year can free up time and energy to focus on your relationships. Cultivating and contributing to healthy relationships in your life—romantic or otherwise—has an enormous positive impact on your health and general well-being.

If all of these areas of your life are a mess and you have to pick one to get started on, start on your health. Having a healthy mind and body can give you the confidence and energy you need to be present and contribute to your relationships. And it goes without saying that doing your job well is much easier when you're healthy and clearheaded.

So, with that in mind, let's do this.

It's better to be hated for who you are than loved for who you are not.

How to Approach This Section

For now, I will spare you all of the science and information behind goal-setting techniques and why writing things down seems to have a "magical" effect on your brain. This is not that kind of journal. I'm just going to tell you flat out: Do these exercises in a quiet place without distractions. Take your time. Don't rush through it.

And remember, life changes. Things happen that are out of your control or that you didn't see coming. Be flexible and adapt as you go along this great journey called life. Don't be hard on yourself if things don't go as planned (they very rarely do anyway).

I'll be giving some brief examples of each step, but it's important that you make this your own process.

Be creative.

Be bold.

Good luck.

Brainstorming

The first step is the easiest and probably the most fun. You'll take twenty minutes to yourself, and write down everything you would like to do in your life before you die. Everything. No matter how big or small, how trivial or important.

Just because you wrote it doesn't mean you have to do it; the point of this step is merely to get your mind exploring—brainstorming.

Write down anything that sounds even remotely cool, remotely possible (or impossible). Anything that sounds like it'd make you excited to wake up in the morning. This should start out very easy but get harder as the time goes by. Hold yourself to twenty minutes! Chances are that during the last five to ten minutes you'll be straining your brain. But keep going anyway.

As you do this first exercise, you may feel yourself get self-conscious or start judging some of your answers. Stop doing this! This list is just between you and yourself. There's absolutely no reason to be ashamed of anything you write. And if you do find yourself hesitant to write too much, perhaps you should ask yourself why you're so scared of accepting many of your own impulses.

On the other hand, chances are, when you're writing your list, two to three entries are going to pop out at you, like giant strobe lights on your page. The specific entries may surprise you as well. This is good.

If you have a lot of surprises on your list or if many of your entries have got you thinking or reconsidering some things already, even better! In fact, if you feel like you're already processing a lot, you may want to take a break for a few hours before the second step.

EXERCISE

Write down everything you would like to do in your life before you die.

- Learn French
- Have Kids
- Experience zero gravity in outer space
- good job
- Steady vehicle
- woke up in general, thankful for that
- I am scared of achieving only because every time I've tried sum bad happens called karma 16. impulses are pretty bad; but all I'm doing is learning from my mistake!
- food in my belly · thankfully
- Roof over my head bc of baby girl
- being un afraid of things I didn't really do before · getting comfortable.
- being a better aunty
- being able to have a great family ♡

- Swim with dolphins
- be a better me
- MAYBE "skydive"
- have my Dream truck!! ♡
- loose more weight
- get jewelry for my future kids
- give my mom what she didnt have, non broken relationship
- 3 more grankids Lmao
- I want people to accept who I really am not just sum good head n pussy bitch

Much Lowkey But damn

Ideal Life (Long-Term)

Now that you've done your brainstorming and come up with more ideas than you'll ever need, it's time to start homing in on what you want your life to look like. Keep in mind, anything is possible with this exercise. We're still fantasizing here. It doesn't matter how possible you feel this life is or isn't, write it down.

Using your imagination will help you tap into some desires that you may not have known were there. Chances are, once you finish this, your mind will already be brainstorming ways to connect the dots from idea to reality. This is good. We've now got your mind working actively to figure out how to achieve your dreams. This is a fundamental first step. You're now motivating yourself based on your own desires and not simply by pleasing others!

amen to being able to open up this far with just myself fr! blessed atmost!

EXERCISE

Describe your ideal life *five years* from now. Describe it in as much detail as possible. Describe where you would live, what you would do each day, what job you'd have, who you'd spend your time with, and what you'd spend your time doing. Take your time. This should take you about twenty minutes.

My ideal life in five years would be me living in California, probably Los Angeles. I'd have my own place near the beach. My work hours would be flexible so I could go surfing often. I'd be focused much more on freelance coding and programming rather than stuck to any individual firm, so I'd have a lot more control over my workload and pay. I'd have a couple kids who would go to a good school. I'd have a lot of time to read, and I'd be in the best physical health of my life. I'd get back into painting and do it from time to time each week, maybe even sell a few of them.

I say don't find yourself. I say never know who you are. Because that's what keeps you striving and discovering. And it forces you to remain humble in your judgments and accepting of the differences in others.

Ideal Life (Short-Term)

This exercise is exactly like the last one, except instead of projecting your ideal life in five years, you are going to project it for one year. This time, make sure your choices are realistic and attainable, but also that they are a step toward your last answer.

EXERCISE

Describe your ideal life *one year* from now. Describe it in as much detail as possible. Describe where you would live, what you would do each day, what job you'd have, who you'd spend your time with, and what you'd spend your time doing. Take your time. This should take you about twenty minutes.

In a year, I will have started my freelance business and will have saved $20K. I'll have invested time and money into getting back into my art and have completed at least three paintings. I'll also have a gym membership and will be working out regularly. Etc.

_____

_____

_____

_____

_____

_____

_____

_____

_____

_____

_____

_____

_____

_____

_____

_____

_____

As you might have noticed, this projection is getting far more actionable. In fact, after you've finished, a lot of the steps you can start taking should be pretty obvious.

You can take a break and come back to this section, but just know that we're not done yet.

Giving the Proper Fucks

Now it's time to really dig into your current life. It's time to look closely at what you're spending your time doing and then root out the activities that aren't serving you or moving you toward your ideal life.

This exercise is a three-parter. First, write down everything you spend your time doing each day. Ignore the small things like brushing your teeth, showering, or sleeping. Focus on the biggies.

Once you can't think of anything else, move to the second column and write down how many hours per week you generally spend doing this activity. If it's something larger like traveling or seasonal like going to White Sox games or something, then just specify that in this column—"two weeks per year," or "ten Saturdays per year," or whatever.

Finally, in the last column, give each item a rating from 1 to 10. This should be based on how much fulfillment you get from that activity. Basically, you are rating how happy that activity makes you.

EXAMPLE:

Activity	Time Spent	Value
Watching TV	15 hours/week	4
Work/Commuting	50 hours/week	3
Watching movies	4 hours/week	6
Hanging out with friends	5 hours/week	8
Browsing the internet	20 hours/week	6

And so on . . .

EXERCISE

Activity	Time Spent	Value

You have a limited amount of fucks to give. Very few, in fact. And if you go around giving a fuck about everything and everyone without conscious thought or choice—well, then you're going to get fucked.

Activity	Time Spent	Value

Activity	Time Spent	Value

Activity	Time Spent	Value

Once you've finished your lists, go back through and look at how the numbers line up. Activities that you spend a lot of time doing should have high numbers. Activities you don't spend much time doing should have low numbers. We're looking for mismatches.

For instance, in the example I gave, two big mismatches pop out at you. The first is that this person really doesn't enjoy their job and they work long hours. That sucks. It's hard to be happy, motivated, and confident when you're dropping fifty hours a week on something you only value at a 3.

The second mismatch is that they're spending two hours a day watching television, but it doesn't deliver much value. Meanwhile, they're averaging less than an hour a day hanging out with friends, something they really value and enjoy.

The answer for this person is clear: ditch the TV to spend more time with friends (or invite your friends over to watch TV with you) and get the job situation figured out.

All this is just from a short, very basic list. Chances are your list has a lot more going on in it.

We don't always control what happens to us. But we always control how we interpret what happens to us, as well as how we respond.

Goals Versus Habits

Okay, so you've just looked at how you currently live your life. You probably noticed that you spend much of your time on activities that aren't very fulfilling. Don't sweat it—that's what we're here for. Our goal, as I'm sure you've guessed by now, is to turn this upside down so you're spending the maximum amount of time possible doing things that make your life awesome.

So we should just design our perfect life and start doing that, right?

Well, not quite.

This is where a lot of people go wrong. They think up a bunch of New Year's resolutions or whatever, then they go hard for like a month or two, and before they know it, they're back to their old behaviors and have forgotten about their goals.

The problem is that most of our behavior is governed by *habits*. Habits are behaviors that are performed automatically, and changing habits is hard. Research shows that trying to change too many habits at once practically always fails.

Instead, in this step, you're going to think of one positive, new habit to install in your life. It takes one to two months of conscious effort for a habit to become ingrained. Once you've created your habit, you can create a new one, until your life is full of awesome, life-improving automatic behaviors. Sounds good, doesn't it?

Six Unsexy Habits That Will Change Your Life

By the way, habits aren't sexy. As I've suggested, they are long-term and repetitive, which makes them seem boring. But achieving lasting change is a boring affair. Here are some key habits that you could, and probably should, introduce into your life.

1. EXERCISE

If you don't know the benefits of regular exercise by now, you must be living under a very large and very old rock.

However, just about everyone overestimates the amount of effort required to get results. Something as simple as briskly walking thirty minutes per day has been shown to lead to vast health improvements and trigger weight loss.

Therefore, if you're starting an exercise habit from scratch, start simple. Worry about the reverse piledriver crunches with your ripped personal trainer named Vlad later.

2. COOKING

This may strike you as a weird one, but I've seen the positive effects of this in too many of my friends' lives to not take it seriously. Most of the benefits don't actually come from the act of cooking itself, but rather they come from the ability to control exactly what and how much you eat.

Eating well, much like exercise, sweeps the board in terms of health and lifestyle benefits: lower risk of obesity, diabetes, various cancers, heart disease and other bad things that kill you; more energy; more focus; better moods (goodbye sugar highs and crashes); better sleep and sex life; among others.

Start with the basics. Make it a goal to cook at least one meal a day. Find healthy recipes that you not only enjoy eating, but also enjoy cooking.

3. MEDITATION

The benefits of meditation are age-old, scientifically proven, and numerous: increased focus, improved self-awareness, reduction of stress and anxiety, improved sleep, greater emotional stability, and more empathy. It can even be used as a form of therapy.

Start with a small daily practice. Even as little as one minute per day can show benefits. I recently discovered an app called Headspace that gently guides people into a meditation practice if you want to learn on your own. Another good one is Calm.

If you find it difficult to meditate (and many people do), find a local group or class. There are often free ones in major cities. It's also a nice way to meet people. Then, once you get the hang of it, try it on your own. Start with one minute per day and slowly work your way up.

4. READING

Reading is fucking magical. It's the only thing in the world that allows you to live inside someone else's brain for a little while, see what they see, feel what they feel, and then leave again.

Studies suggest that people who read regularly are far more empathetic. They care about other people more. They relate and respond to others better. People who read regularly are also smarter, better informed, and more knowledgeable about the world than those who don't.

When developing a reading habit, start with what seems easy and exciting to you, then slowly branch out. If you like teen murder mysteries even though you're a forty-five-year-old single mother, read teen murder mysteries. If you like books about zombies, read books about zombies.

And here's another tip: if you aren't enjoying a book, *stop reading it*.

I meet so many people who hate a book they're reading, yet they begrudgingly drag themselves back to it over and over again because they feel bad if they don't finish. This is crazy.

My rule of thumb is, when I start reading a book, I force myself to read the first 10 percent. And if I don't like it by the end of that, I put it down and move on to the next book.

5. WRITING

If reading allows you to inhabit other people's minds for a brief period of time, learning to write well is like cleaning your house before the guests come over—it forces you to learn how to structure your thoughts more coherently, string together rational arguments, and tell stories in cogent and insightful ways. It's also therapeutic.

The easiest way here is to start a journal. There are some cool apps. Or you can do it the old-fashioned way, by hand.

The important thing is to not limit yourself. Use writing as a tool of self-discovery—write your feelings, ideas, fantasies. If you feel like going on a tangent about calculus problems that stumped you, do that too.

6. SOCIALIZING

I know it sounds painfully obvious, but having friends is fucking serious. I think many of us, if we slow down long enough to take a look at ourselves, don't give our relationships the time or attention necessary to keep them healthy and happy.

It turns out loneliness is kind of a thing. It's growing at an alarming rate in the US, particularly among older people. And new research is discovering that being alone can be just as bad for your physical health as obesity or heavy smoking.

Here's something simple you can do: make a point to talk to a different friend every single day.

Now, I don't mean just bullshitty Facebook chatter. I mean genuine, "Hey man, what's been going on with you lately? How have things been?" followed by a couple, "Oh, that's cool, tell me about that," and finally finished off with a, "We should get together soon, what are you doing next week?" for good measure. It would take maybe fifteen to twenty minutes at most.

You'll be surprised by how easy it is to connect with many people. You'll be much happier for it.

If you wish to be loved, then love. If you wish to be appreciated, then appreciate. If you wish to be respected, then respect.

How to Create a Habit

Habits form when you engage in a behavior *repeatedly in the presence of consistent stimuli*. That last part is important. Habits are "automatic" responses to familiar environmental cues. You save mental energy by developing habitual responses to familiar cues, situations, and even people who you encounter on a regular basis.

Countless studies have shown that habits consist of three main parts: an environmental cue, a behavioral response, and a reward (or the removal of an unpleasant stimulus).

CUE → BEHAVIOR → REWARD

For example, if you're a smoker, your cravings are typically triggered by a cue that you associate with smoking. For instance, finishing a big meal, drinking a beer, or seeing someone smoking a cigarette on TV.

This cue then triggers your desire to perform the habitual behavior. Then you smoke, and your brain rewards you—you feel more relaxed, calmer (and, of course, the nicotine helps as well).

Habit researchers have found that in order to create new habits (or break old ones), we should *not* focus on the behavior but rather focus on the cue.

The "reward" component of the habit equation above is used to reinforce your target behavior after you've successfully completed it.

During the first month or two of forming a new habit, you consciously have to repeat the behavior. After a while, the pattern will become ingrained in your brain, and eventually, you will perform it practically automatically.

EXERCISE

Think of a new behavior you'd like to make a habit. Then think of a cue for that behavior and a way to reward yourself after performing the behavior. If the behavior itself is already rewarding for you, then the reward isn't necessary.

Make sure you specify a cue, a behavior, and a reward.

EXAMPLE:

When watching my favorite show, I have to stop and do at least 10 pushups or situps before each episode. I'm not allowed to watch each episode until I've done 10 pushups or situps.

YOUR NEW HABIT #1

_____

_____

DATE IT BECAME A HABIT

_____

YOUR NEW HABIT #2

_____

_____

DATE IT BECAME A HABIT

_____

YOUR NEW HABIT #3

_____
_____
_____
_____
_____

DATE IT BECAME A HABIT

_____

YOUR NEW HABIT #4

_____
_____
_____
_____
_____

DATE IT BECAME A HABIT

_____

YOUR NEW HABIT #5

_____
_____
_____
_____
_____
_____

DATE IT BECAME A HABIT

_____

YOUR NEW HABIT #6

_____
_____
_____
_____
_____
_____

DATE IT BECAME A HABIT

_____

YOUR NEW HABIT #7

_____

_____

_____

_____

_____

_____

DATE IT BECAME A HABIT

_____

YOUR NEW HABIT #8

_____

_____

_____

_____

_____

_____

DATE IT BECAME A HABIT

_____

YOUR NEW HABIT #9

_____

_____

_____

_____

_____

_____

DATE IT BECAME A HABIT

_____

YOUR NEW HABIT #10

_____

_____

_____

_____

_____

_____

DATE IT BECAME A HABIT

_____

FIND GREATER PURPOSE

Your Action Plan

From the previous steps in this section, you should have developed a pretty clear idea of what you need to be doing differently, both in the short-term and in the long-term. You've likely been made aware of things that you'd like to have in your life that you currently don't. And maybe you've identified some things that you have in your life, but you'd prefer you didn't.

You should also now understand how goals are best leveraged as part of a system of habits.

The final step will be to develop a system that will help you bridge the gap between where you are now and where you want to be in the long run—that is, your ideal life.

The next exercise will bring together everything from this section. We will start by reviewing what you wrote in the second exercise when you envisioned your ideal life five years from now, and identifying three to five of the broad, long-term goals in your description.

Let's look back at the example I provided for that exercise:

My ideal life in five years would be me living in California, probably Los Angeles. I'd have my own place near the beach. My work hours would be flexible so I could go surfing often. I'd be focused much more on freelance coding and programming rather than stuck to any individual firm, so I'd have a lot more control over my workload and pay. I'd have a couple kids who would go to a good school. I'd have a lot of time to read, and I'd be in the best physical health of my life. I'd get back into painting and do it from time to time each week, maybe even sell a few of them.

Notice how you can pick out broad goals from this description:

1. More professional freedom (flexible work hours through running a business)
2. Starting a family (kids)
3. Improved health (best physical health of my life)
4. Painting

We're going to create a system that will get us closer to these broad, long-term goals. The way we do this is by breaking each goal down into smaller, more manageable parts across more manageable time frames.

So, what's *one thing you can* do this year to get you closer to one of these five-year goals? Then, what's *one thing* you can do this month to put you on track to achieving your yearly goal? What's *one thing* you can do this week to put you on track to achieving your monthly goal?

And finally, what's one thing you can do today to put you on track to achieving your goal for the week, which puts you on track to achieving your goal for the month, which puts you on track to achieving your goal for the year, which puts you on track to achieving your goal for the next five years?

EXAMPLE:

Sticking to the example I provided, the three broad, long-term goals I identified were:

1. More professional freedom (flexible work hours through running a business)
2. Starting a family (kids)
3. Improved health (best physical shape of my life)

I'll break these down to give you an example of how I'd do this.

Long-term goal	Run a profitable business and be financially independent
1-year goal	$25k+ from my coding side business
1-month goal	Get 2 new clients
1-week goal	Pitch 10 leads
Daily habit/action	Research and call/email 2 leads per day

Long-term goal	Start a family
1-year goal	Find a partner
1-month goal	Go on three dates
1-week goal	Hang out with a new group of people for one night
Daily habit/action	Start a conversation with at least one stranger every day: face-to-face, dating apps/site, social media, etc.

Long-term goal	Be in the best physical health of my life
1-year goal	Lose 20 pounds
1-month goal	Lose 4 pounds
1-week goal	Exercise 5 times per week
Daily habit/action	Minimum 30 minutes of daily movement: gym/kickboxing, push-ups/sit-ups/pull-ups, bike ride, jog, etc.

When you're done with this exercise, you should have the backbone of your system with three to five goals to work toward over the next year. Remember, start with *one* goal-habit combination, and after about a month or so, you can re-evaluate and adjust. Move on to the next habit if it's going well or adjust your daily action if it needs some fine-tuning to keep you on track.

EXERCISE: CREATE YOUR ACTION PLANS

Fill out an action plan below for each of your goals. If you run out of action plans, you can create new ones in the notes section at the back. You can create multiple plans for each goal (stick to about three to five for now).

ACTION PLAN #1

Long-term goal	
1-year goal	
1-month goal	
1-week goal	
Daily habit/action	

ACTION PLAN #2

Long-term goal	
1-year goal	
1-month goal	
1-week goal	
Daily habit/ action	

ACTION PLAN #3

Long-term goal	
1-year goal	
1-month goal	
1-week goal	
Daily habit/ action	

Self-love is usually unpleasant and boring. Saving for retirement is self-love. Going to bed early is self-love. Eating a goddamn salad is self-love.

ACTION PLAN #4

Long-term goal	
1-year goal	
1-month goal	
1-week goal	
Daily habit/ action	

ACTION PLAN #5

Long-term goal	
1-year goal	
1-month goal	
1-week goal	
Daily habit/ action	

ACTION PLAN #6

Long-term goal	
1-year goal	
1-month goal	
1-week goal	
Daily habit/ action	

ACTION PLAN #7

Long-term goal	
1-year goal	
1-month goal	
1-week goal	
Daily habit/ action	

Just because something's not your fault doesn't mean it's not your responsibility. Our ability to act and change is proportional to the amount of responsibility we take on for ourselves.

ACTION PLAN #8

Long-term goal	
1-year goal	
1-month goal	
1-week goal	
Daily habit/ action	

ACTION PLAN #9

Long-term goal	
1-year goal	
1-month goal	
1-week goal	
Daily habit/ action	

ACTION PLAN #10

Long-term goal	
1-year goal	
1-month goal	
1-week goal	
Daily habit/ action	

You don't build psychological resilience by feeling good all the time. You build psychological resilience by getting better at feeling bad.

CONGRATULATIONS, YOU'RE DONE!

If you've completed everything in this section, you should now have

- a clearer long-term vision of what you want your life to look like;
- some definable, actionable goals to complete within the next year; and
- a starting place to begin moving toward those goals.

Like I said in the beginning, I recommend repeating this exercise each year. In my experience, it's normal to meet most, but not all of the goals you set each year if you keep on top of them. Maybe two out of three or so.

The more goals you achieve, the easier it'll become to achieve subsequent goals. That's the beauty of all of this. Discipline is a skill. If you exercise it, it gets stronger. Achieving goals based on your internal desires and motivations builds self-esteem and increases your motivation in the future.

If you do these exercises consistently for a few years, you'll realize that your priorities change with time. What you may consider very important today may not seem as important a year from now.

Doing this sets off a chain reaction, and if you follow it long enough, implementing change into your life will become easier and easier. One day, years from now, you'll look back, and maybe you won't even recognize the person you are now.

And that'll be a good thing.

A FEW PAGES OF SPACE TO WRITE DOWN VARIOUS PERSONAL REALIZATIONS

A FEW PAGES OF SPACE TO WRITE DOWN VARIOUS PERSONAL REALIZATIONS

A FEW PAGES OF SPACE TO WRITE DOWN VARIOUS PERSONAL REALIZATIONS

A FEW PAGES OF SPACE TO WRITE DOWN VARIOUS PERSONAL REALIZATIONS

A FEW PAGES OF SPACE TO WRITE DOWN VARIOUS PERSONAL REALIZATIONS

A FEW PAGES OF SPACE TO WRITE DOWN VARIOUS PERSONAL REALIZATIONS

A FEW PAGES OF SPACE TO WRITE DOWN VARIOUS PERSONAL REALIZATIONS

A FEW PAGES OF SPACE TO WRITE DOWN VARIOUS PERSONAL REALIZATIONS

Acknowledgments

Special thanks to Jessica O'Reilly for all of her help putting this journal together. I'd also like to thank Drew Birnie and Philip Kemper for their assistance coming up with a few of the exercises here.

About the Author

Mark Manson is a two-time #1 *New York Times* bestselling author whose books have sold over fourteen million copies worldwide. His work has been translated into more than sixty-five languages and hit bestseller lists in sixteen different countries. Mark Manson maintains a blog and newsletter, which are read by over a million people each month. He currently lives in Los Angeles.

More from Me

BOOKS

I am the #1 *New York Times* bestselling author of *The Subtle Art of Not Giving a F*ck* and *Everything is F*cked: A Book About Hope*.

COMPANION TO THIS JOURNAL

OTHER BOOK

MINDF*CK MONTHLY

Interested in starting each week full of ideas that could potentially change your life? Sign up for my newsletter, lovingly called "Mindf*ck Monthly," because, well, we all need a little attitude on Monday morning.

markmanson.net/newsletter

THE SUBTLE ART SCHOOL

Join millions of readers around the world by visiting **school.markmanson.net**, where you'll find life advice that is science-based, pragmatic, and non-bullshitty—aka, life advice that doesn't suck. Some people say I'm an idiot. Other people say I saved their life. Visit markmanson.net and decide for yourself.

SOCIAL MEDIA

@markmanson
@iammarkmanson
@Markmansonnet